FREEDOM FORCES

★ U.S. SPECIAL OPERATIONS ★ COMMAND

FORCE AGAINST TERRORISTS

Tom Greve

Rourke
Educational Media
rourkeeducationalmedia.com

www.rourkeeducationalmedia.com

PHOTO CREDITS: Cover photo courtesy U.S. Marine Corps; back cover and title page: flag © SFerdon; red background on pages © Eky Studio Page 4 courtesy U.S. Army; Page 6 courtesy defenseimagery.mil; Page 7 courtesy U.S. Navy; Pages 8/9 courtesy U.S. Militaryphotos by Mass Communication Specialist 2nd Class Christopher Menzie, Mass Communication Specialist 2nd Class Shauntae Hinkle-Lymas, Pfc. Laura M. Bigenho, Tech. Sgt. Keith Brown; Page 10 courtesy National Archives and Records Administration; Page 11 courtesy Library and Archives Canada, map © ildogesto; Page 12/13 courtesy U.S. Navy photo by Mass Communication Specialist 2nd Class Kyle D. Gahlau; Page 14 courtesy German Federal Archive; Page 16 © Michael Foran; Page 17 courtesy U.S. Government; Page 18 courtesy U.S. Navy; Page 19 © Robert F. Balazik; Page 20 courtesy U.S. Army photo by Petty Officer 2nd Class Katrina Beeler; Page 21 courtesy DVIDSHUB photo by Emmanuel Rios; Pages 22/23 courtesy U.S. Army, photos by Cpl. Peter R. Miller and Cpl. Christopher O'Quin; Page 24 © Osama Bin Laden photo courtesy FBI, map © pavalena; Page 25 courtesy U.S. Government; Page 26 © Truthdowser; Page 27 courtesy U.S. Navy, photos by Gunnery Sergeant Shannon Arledge of the 2nd Marine Aircraft Wing; Page 29 courtesy U.S. Navy photo by Chief Mass Communication Specialist Kathryn Whittenberger

Edited by Precious McKenzie

Designed and Produced by Blue Door Publishing, FL

Library of Congress Cataloging-in-Publication Data

U.S. Special Operations Command: Force Against Terrorists / Tom Greve
  p. cm. -- (Freedom Forces)
  ISBN 978-1-62169-927-9 (hard cover) (alk. paper)
  ISBN 978-1-62169-822-7 (soft cover)
  ISBN 978-1-62717-031-4 (e-book)
Library of Congress Control Number: 2013938879

Also Available as:
ROURKE'S
e-Books

Rourke Educational Media
Printed in the United States of America,
North Mankato, Minnesota

Rourke
Educational Media

rourkeeducationalmedia.com
customerservice@rourkeeducationalmedia.com
PO Box 643328 Vero Beach, Florida 32964

TABLE OF CONTENTS

CHAPTER ONE
SPECIAL OPERATIONS COMMAND:
AMERICA'S FIT FIGHTING FORCE

In the cold dark of a starless night, a U.S. soldier crouches silently behind a wall. His heart beats like a kick drum as he waits for word to move forward. His breathing and concentration are controlled and steady. He is **poised**, ready to receive an order and carry it out with deadly force.

This is no actor in some action movie. This is a Special Operations soldier. A person trained to carry out difficult, dangerous missions nearly anywhere on Earth with a steady hand, a clear mind, and an iron will. The purpose of a Special Operations soldier is to protect the country against hidden and secretive enemies.

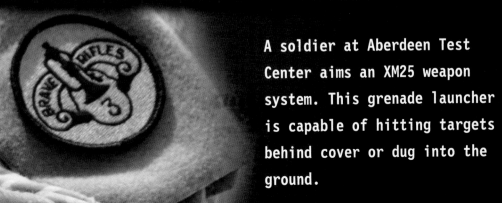

A soldier at Aberdeen Test Center aims an XM25 weapon system. This grenade launcher is capable of hitting targets behind cover or dug into the ground.

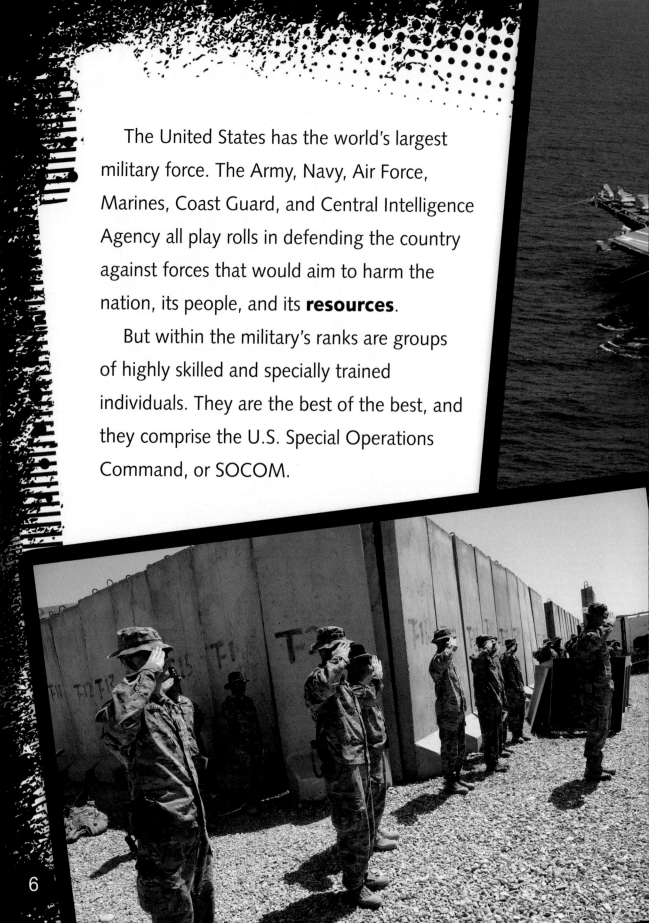

The United States has the world's largest military force. The Army, Navy, Air Force, Marines, Coast Guard, and Central Intelligence Agency all play rolls in defending the country against forces that would aim to harm the nation, its people, and its **resources**.

But within the military's ranks are groups of highly skilled and specially trained individuals. They are the best of the best, and they comprise the U.S. Special Operations Command, or SOCOM.

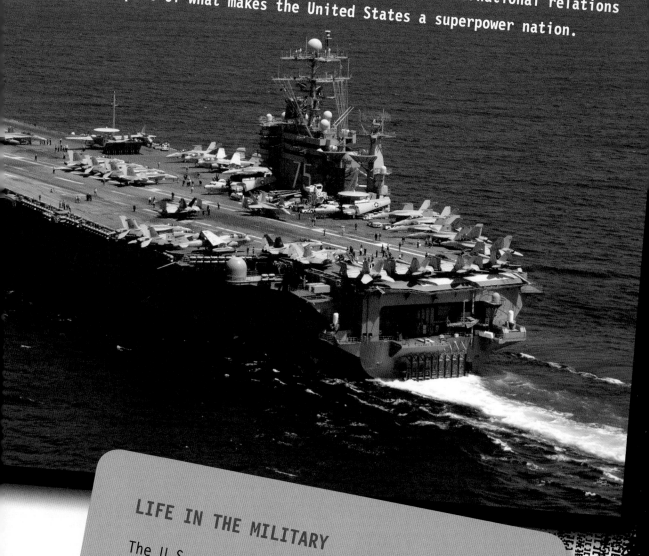

The sheer size of the U.S. defense force, its annual budget, and its wide-reaching capabilities to influence international relations are part of what makes the United States a superpower nation.

LIFE IN THE MILITARY

The U.S. military relies on a specific chain of command to streamline nearly everything it does. There is little tolerance for individual or selfish action. All members operate according to a code of conduct. This means soldiers follow orders from superiors without question. The military operates this way in peacetime as well as during times of war.

Members of Special Operations Command are especially tough. They have to be able to deal with fatigue, discomfort, and even pain, all while working in harsh conditions without losing focus on their mission.

Soldiers applying for SOCOM units have to pass demanding physical tests to show strength, endurance, and a high level of physical fitness. These include swimming long distances in uniform, hiking with heavy loads at night, and distance running, all performed in a short amount of time.

But it's not just physical toughness that qualifies a soldier for special operations duty. The person's strength has to be matched by smarts.

WOMEN AND THE SPECIAL FORCES.

Women are a valuable part of the Special Operations Command. They have traditionally filled support roles like language interpreters, pilots, or medical staff, though they may soon see their range of responsibility, and their demand, increase. As of 2013, the U.S. military gave women clearance to serve in combat roles. This could open the door to women serving in the most elite Special Operations Command combat units like the Army's Delta Force or the Navy's SEALs, which remain all male. Overall, women make up about 14 percent of the 1.4 million people serving in the U.S. armed forces.

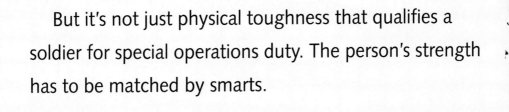

14 %
female

86 % male

CHAPTER TWO SOCOM's HISTORY:

MATCHING MIGHT TO THE MISSION

The United States military began training special operations forces during World War II. After the surprise 1941 bombing attack on the U.S. military base at Pearl Harbor, Hawaii by Japan, the U.S. sent soldiers, sailors, and marines off to fight in World War II. The places overseas where the war raged, called theaters, had wildly different **environments**, climates, and enemy tactics.

On the morning of December 7, 1941, the Japanese launched a surprise air attack on the U.S. Naval Base at Pearl Harbor in Hawaii. Outraged, the U.S. declared war the following day, bringing the United States into World War II.

The first special forces unit was called the Devil's Brigade. Formed in 1942, they were specially chosen U.S. and Canadian soldiers trained to operate and fight against Nazi Germany in Europe's most extreme mountainous areas as well as against Japanese forces in the Aleutian Islands of Alaska. Skilled at parachuting, skiing, and hand-to-hand combat, the Devil's Brigade played a key role in helping the U.S. and its **allied** forces win the war.

The Devil's Brigade were also called the Black Devils because they smeared their faces with black boot polish during night operations.

Aleutian Islands

CANADA

UNITED STATES

Greenland (Denmark)

Germany

Iceland

France

Spain

Algeria

Mauritania

Mali

Gulf of Mexico

Venezuela

Military commanders soon understood the advantage of a smaller, specially trained force operating in a separate but coordinated way with the Army, Navy, Air Force, and Marine Corps. Smaller forces could move quickly and strike fast.

Since World War II, the nature of military combat has grown even more complicated. Not just in terms of battlefields and equipment, but also in terms of the nature of the United States' enemies and their fighting tactics.

MAJOR U.S. MILITARY CONFLICTS SINCE

1941-1945	1950-1953	1965-1973
World War II	Korean War	Vietnam War

DRAFT VS VOLUNTEER

From World War I until the end of the Vietnam War, the U.S. used drafts to build up the staffing of its military during wartime. That meant all young men could be selected for **mandatory** service in the country's armed forces. Since 1973, men and women volunteer to serve, including Special Operations Command forces.

Some elite Special Operations units are trained to be amphibious, meaning they are skilled at combat on land or at sea.

PEARL HARBOR (DECEMBER 7, 1941)

1990-1991

2001-PRESENT

2003-2009

Gulf War
(Iraq Desert Storm)

Afghanistan

Iraq

World War II unfolded on multiple continents and across the Pacific Ocean against enemies fighting by mostly traditional militaries.

Panzer VI (Tiger I) German Tank

Both Germany and Japan had uniformed armys, navys, and air forces that battled the U.S. and its allies throughout World War II.

Imperial Japanese Navy's battle ship, *Yamato*

In the decades since the U.S. won World War II, the U.S. has fought wars against increasingly irregular military enemies skilled at **guerrilla** combat tactics and **terrorism**.

THE VIETNAM WAR

Special Operations units were in Vietnam years before the rest of the U.S. military. They worked to train Vietnamese soldiers in guerilla combat tactics against enemy forces from North Vietnam. The U.S. eventually became heavily involved in the Vietnam War, creating widespread and sometimes violent disagreement among the American people and the U.S. government over the proper role of the U.S. military in foreign affairs. Those arguments continue to this very day.

Perhaps no single event had a greater impact on the role and scope of the U.S. Special Operations Command than the terrorist attacks of September 11, 2001. Like Pearl Harbor in 1941, the September 11, 2001 terrorist attack on the U.S. was a surprise. But, unlike Pearl Harbor, the enemy behind 9/11 was not a nation with a regular fighting force. Rather, it was the murderous work of secretive terrorists wanting to harm the U.S. for perceived injustices. The U.S. faced an invisible enemy rather than an enemy nation or army.

SEPTEMBER 11, 2001

While the U.S. responded to Pearl Harbor with massive military action across the globe, the response to 9/11 has put the expertise of Special Operations Command forces front and center in the nation's overall military defense plan.

The coordinated attacks, carried out by terrorists **hijacking** commercial airplanes and crashing them into New York City's World Trade Center and the Pentagon in Washington, D.C. were in some ways like the horrific experience of Pearl Harbor all over again.

America's Special Operations Command forces have grown in number since the days of the Devil's Brigade. Today's SOCOM includes approximately 60,000 active duty members. They include units from all of the major branches of the U.S. Armed Forces.

In 2013 the head of U.S. Special Operations Command was Admiral William McRaven. All Special Operations Command forces from the four major service branches report up the chain of command to him. He, in turn, reports to the President of the United States.

SOCOM (Special Operations Command)

Admiral McRaven

ARMY	NAVY	AIR FORCE	MARINES
On Land	By Sea	By Air	First To Fight
Delta Force/ Rangers	SEALs Sea, Air, and Land	AFSOC Air Force Special Operations	MARSOC Marine Special Operations Command

OPERATION EAGLE CLAW

The military decided to unify the various Special Operations branches under the command of SOCOM after an ill-fated 1980 attempt to rescue American hostages in Iran. A helicopter crash left 8 servicemen dead and a follow-up investigation found lack of coordinated planning between the military branches was at least partly to blame. The failed mission, known as Operation Eagle Claw, remains among the worst special operations tragedies in U.S. history.

UNITED STATES

IRAN

CHAPTER THREE
SOCOM SINCE 9/11:
THE NEW NORMAL

In the years since September 11, 2001, the U.S. has been involved in two major conflicts overseas. First, the U.S. invaded Afghanistan to wage war on suspected terrorist groups involved in the planning of the 9/11 attacks. The War in Afghanistan continues in 2013.

The U.S. also invaded Iraq in 2003. Although U.S. combat operations in Iraq stopped in 2010, these conflicts have caused Special Operations Command to expand.

During the wars in Iraq and Afghanistan, Special Operations personnel increasingly work as partners with local police and civilians, trying to identify those working in secret against the U.S. The military calls this work counterinsurgency.

THE FIVE TRUTHS OF SPECIAL OPERATIONS COMMAND

1. **HUMANS ARE MORE IMPORTANT THAN HARDWARE.**

2. **QUALITY IS BETTER THAN QUANTITY.**
   (A few specially trained fighters are more effective than a large force of untrained fighters)

3. **PROPERLY TRAINED SPECIAL OPERATIONS FORCES CANNOT BE MASS-PRODUCED.**
   (Training special forces soldiers, sailors, and marines takes time and effort. There are no shortcuts to being ready for success in combat or other operations)

4. **COMPETENT SPECIAL OPERATIONS FORCES CANNOT BE CREATED AFTER EMERGENCIES OCCUR.**
   (That's too late. Their preparation makes them ready to deal with the emergency as it happens)

5. **MOST SPECIAL OPERATIONS REQUIRE ASSISTANCE FROM THE ARMY, NAVY, AIR FORCE, OR MARINES.**
   (Special Operations Command is like the tip of a spear. The tip hits its target first, but it's the whole spear behind it that constitutes the weapon. So too, does the U.S. military constitute the country's overall fighting force)

In the years since the 9/11 attack, the number of Special Operations Command personnel has doubled. Its budget, or the money set aside by the U.S. Department of Defense to pay for the selection, training, and **deployment** of personnel, has tripled. Simply put, special operations have never been more important to the defense of the nation than they are today. This means talented, smart, and tough young adults will continually be in demand to fill the needs of this vital part of the U.S. military.

THE MILITARY INDUSTRIAL COMPLEX

Former President Dwight Eisenhower served as commander of the European theater during World War II, becoming arguably the greatest American military hero of the past century. As president however, he warned against placing too much value in military strength. He felt the cost of large-scale weapons and a massive military took money away from other national needs like education. His argument, which he called the Military Industrial Complex, remains a part of American politics to this very day.

President
Dwight Eisenhower
(1890-1969)

SOCOM'S MISSION STATEMENT

Provide fully capable Special Operations forces to defend the United States and its interests. Synchronize planning of global operations against terrorist networks.

CHAPTER FOUR

HIGH STAKES TRIUMPHS

Nearly a decade after the U.S. first went into Afghanistan to find the terrorist leaders responsible for the September 11 attack, the group's leader, Osama bin Laden, was tracked to a village not in Afghanistan, but in neighboring Pakistan.

This highlighted the irregular nature of the war against terrorists. U.S. commanders could not launch a full military operation in Pakistan. So, to get bin Laden, they sent in a top secret Special Operations Command Unit specifically trained in **precision** combat tactics: Navy Seal Team 6.

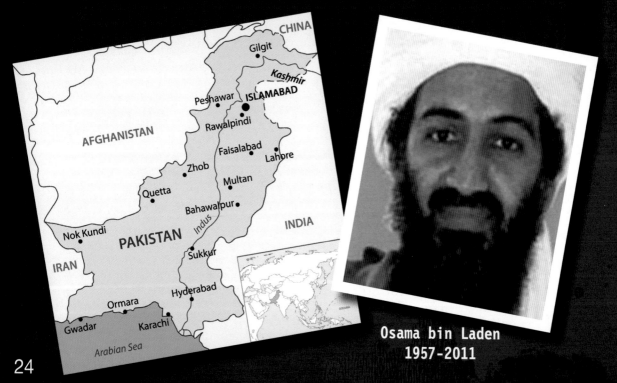

Osama bin Laden
1957-2011

In May of 2011, about two dozen SEALs flew in two helicopters in the middle of the night from a U.S. air base in Afghanistan to bin Laden's suspected hiding spot in Pakistan.

The directive for the SEALs to capture or kill bin Laden came from President Barack Obama.

The President also holds the title Commander-in-Chief of all U.S. armed forces.

In the course of just 40 minutes, the SEALs, operating in pitch-black darkness, found bin Laden, killed him and several of his armed associates, collected his body along with evidence they found in his house and flew back to the Afghan base. Mission accomplished.

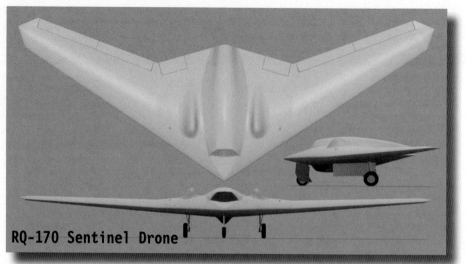

RQ-170 Sentinel Drone

Much of what SOCOM commanders knew about bin Laden's hiding place was gathered by surveillance drones, which had flown overhead. These controversial unmanned spy planes are small, quiet, and hard to detect on radar but can provide clear images of landscapes or specific buildings.

SNIPER RESCUE MISSION

Special Operations snipers from the Navy SEALs were also involved in the 2009 kidnapping rescue of the captain of the cargo ship *Maersk Alabama*. The snipers, in a lifeboat being towed by a Navy ship, shot three captors dead from long range and the kidnapped captain was safely rescued.

Advances in weapons technology combined with the steely resolve of a well-trained Special Operations Command force make the modern U.S. military the greatest national defense organization the world has ever seen.

The U.S. Special Operations Command is comprised of the fittest of the fit. They are top-notch military fighters specially trained for dangerous duty against secretive terrorist organizations and other dangers. Their role in the overall military has grown in response to the threat of terrorism. Whether from the Army, Navy, Air Force, or Marines, Special Operations fighters use their intense training to defend the country and its interests around the world.

The lifeboat where four Somali pirates held Captain Richard Phillips hostage was identified using a U.S. Navy Scan Eagle UAV.

TIMELINE

1942:
Devil's Brigade members scale mountains in winter to defeat surprised Nazi forces at Italy's Monte Le Difensa.

1961:
President Kennedy refers to the green hats worn by the Army's Special Forces as a fitting emblem of the courage and achievement of the American military. Army Special Forces soldiers become popularly known as Green Berets.

1980s:
New testing qualifications make it even tougher to gain acceptance into Special Forces duty.

1957:
Special Operations Units begin training South Vietnamese soldiers in tactical combat long before conventional U.S. forces enter the fight. The first American killed in Vietnam is Special Forces Captain Harry Kramer.

1972:
The last American to die in Vietnam is Special Forces Sergeant Fred Mack.

1987:
Following an extensive military review, all Special Operations Forces are centralized under the leadership of the Special Operations Command.

1989:

Army's Delta Force rescues an American from Panamanian prison during brief U.S. invasion to oust Manuel Noriega.

2001-present:

Special Operations Command take leadership role in counterinsurgency efforts after U.S. invasions of Afghanistan and Iraq.

2011:

After a decade-long manhunt, Navy SEAL Team 6 finds and kills suspected mastermind of September 11 attack Osama bin Laden in daring night raid in Pakistan.

2001:

September 11 terrorist attacks on U.S.

2009:

Navy SEAL snipers shoot and kill Somali terrorists holding an American cargo ship captain hostage at sea. The captain is freed.

SHOW WHAT YOU KNOW

1. Which branches of the military contribute to Special Operations?

2. Describe the types of missions Special Operations perform.

3. How did Special Operations find Osama bin Laden?

4. Describe the types of careers people have in the military.

5. Explain how Special Operations keeps America safe from terrorism.

GLOSSARY

allied (AL-ide): groups joining together to battle a common enemy

deployment (de-PLOY-muhnt): to send a military force or weapon into position for action

environments (en-VYE-ruhn-muhntss): the places and surroundings in which a person works

guerrilla (guh-RIL-uh): a small group of hidden fighters using surprise tactics against an army

hijacking (HYE-jak-ing): the forceful takeover of an airplane to change its destination

mandatory (MAN-dih-TOR-ee): required, not optional

poised (POIZD): composed, in control of one's own thinking and actions

precision (pre-SIH-zhuhn): exact, without error or shortcoming

resources (RE-sor-sez): things of value to a place or nation, such as land, materials, and fossil fuels

terrorism (TER-uhr-izm): to frighten with violent acts in order to affect change

Index

Websites to Visit

http://www.americanspecialops.com
http://www.military.com/special-operations
hhtp://www.socom.mil

About the Author

Tom Greve lives in Chicago. He is married, has two children, and enjoys reading and writing about military history. He has an older brother who served six years in the U.S. Navy. He is grateful to all who have served in the U.S. military.

Meet The Author!
www.meetREMauthors.com

Per RFP 03764 Follett School Solutions guarantees
hardcover bindings through SY 2024-2025
877.899.8550 or customerservice@follett.com